Narayana Murthy

N Chokkan

Narayana Murthy
© *New Horizon Media*

First Edition: July 2009
64 Pages
Printed in India.

ISBN 978-81-8493-193-8
Pro-ya-en-46

Prodigy Books
177/103, First Floor,
Ambal's Building, Lloyds Road,
Royapettah, Chennai 600 014.
Ph: +91-44-4200-9603

Email : support@nhm.in
Website : www.nhm.in

Prodigy Books is an imprint of New Horizon Media Private Limited

Contents

A burning desire

There were seven of them. And all of them were employees of Patni Computer Services (PCS) in Mumbai. They shared a dream…

Experts in computer technology, all seven believed that the software industry had a great future at the global level. Anyone grasping this opportunity could earn wealth by fair and honest means. But to those seven men, money was secondary.

What encouraged them was their anxiety that India could miss the information revolution. Indians were experts in the field. If they made all the right moves with careful planning, they could bring laurels to the country. But this could not happen overnight. They had to work towards their goal in a patient and unhurried manner, without being lured by the desire for instant results.

To realise their dreams and to concentrate on their long-term plans, they needed an open mind, freedom and hard work, and the most important of all, the conviction that they could do it. All the seven had all these qualities. But they had other problems too, the most important being lack of money! Their aim was to establish a new software business of global standards, but they did not have the capital.

One of the seven was Narayana Murthy, who headed the software section of Patni. He had discussed his long-cherished plans for a new software company with some of his colleagues who thought alike and agreed to be part of his new venture. But it was impossible to start a software business with just a meeting of minds and high principles. Each of the partners had to save considerable money to invest in the dream venture.

Money had always been a problem for Narayana Murthy since his childhood. He was often lost in thought about the lack of adequate finance which stood between him and his dream.

Focussed on academics

Narayana Murthy was born on 20 August, 1946, a year before India became independent, in a poor Brahmin family in the erstwhile Sidlagatta of Mysore State. His father Nagavara Rama Rao was a high school teacher who taught mathematics and biology. He had eight children—five daughters and three sons, including Narayana Murthy. Being the sole breadwinner, it was not easy for him to run the family.

However, Rao's profession helped his children understand the importance of education. As a child, Murthy learnt from his parents through word and deed that it was not important to earn money or have a lavish lifestyle, but to study well and improve your knowledge about the world. He also learnt not to be selfish but think of the society's welfare instead. 'Never tell a lie,' they told him, 'always follow the path of truth and be ready for all kinds of sacrifices.'

Despite difficulties, Rao ensured that his children received good education. Murthy did well at school, showed great enthusiasm and often won laurels as a good student. Next to his parents, it was his teachers that Murthy admired the most. Love for studies came naturally to him and his respect for his teachers made him study his lessons with devotion.

Even at a very young age, he understood that being poor was not something to be ashamed of. Everyday, he learnt the intricacies of contented living, and with dignity, which continue to help him even today.

When Murthy's family lived in Mandya near Mysore, they bought timber dust for fuel from a local trader. He in turn brought it from a timber depot located at a distance. Murthy's mother reasoned out that if someone from the family fetched it directly from the depot, it would cost much less. Why worry when there are three sons at home, she thought.

She offered Murthy and his brothers some payment if they agreed to bring the timber dust from the depot. The boys were too willing and immediately consented to it. They took turns riding their father's bicycle to the depot and bought the dust at a cheaper rate. They spent the tips they earned from this errand, on eats. Only such small pleasures kept them going at that young age.

A bright student in school, Murthy had great aptitude for science and mathematics, and quickly grasped whatever was taught in the classroom. This made him very popular among his classmates who constantly pestered him for clearing their doubts. He vividly explained to them with great patience, a trait that drew him to the teaching profession later in life. Not only his classmates but also his seniors came to him with their doubts and often got certain points clarified.

Murthy stood first in his class every year. In the 10th Standard Examination, Murthy scored the fourth highest marks in the State and was quite thrilled with his rank. But his father was a little disappointed and asked his son, 'Only the fourth rank? What happened to the first three ranks?' By voicing his unhappiness with the results, Rao was only trying to inspire Murthy to do better.

Murthy felt as if a door had been thrown open to him suddenly. After that, he always tried to be the best in whatever he did. He would tell himself, 'I want to be the first—anything below that is for others.'

Dream and Reality

Narayana Murthy's parents had great dreams and expectations for their son's future. A close relative of Murthy was employed in government service and Rao wanted Murthy to get into a similar job. But Murthy was not too keen on that. Interested as he was in science and mathematics, he wanted to pursue engineering at the prestigious Indian Institute of Technology. It was his dream to get into IIT and achieve something big there.

But it was tough to get into IIT. The marks scored in the school public examination did not count for admission into IIT, and it was based purely on the rank obtained in a competitive all-India entrance examination the institute held annually, with several thousand students competing for just over a thousand seats.

Nothing deterred Murthy. He firmly believed that everytime he ran into a problem he could overcome it by working harder. When the results were announced, Murthy was ranked 17th among the thousands of candidates from all over India. But Murthy's dream was shattered when his father dropped a bombshell. He simply said, 'No Murthy, you cannot join the IIT.'

'Why father?' asked Murthy with trepidation.

His father replied, 'Don't you know our financial situation?'

Rama Rao earned a meagre Rs. 250 a month those days, and he had to feed the family, educate all the children and get his daughters married with this modest income. Under such circumstances, he did not believe he could afford the expenditure on Murthy's IIT education.

Rama Rao knew that Murthy's dream was to study at the IIT. Nevertheless, given the family situation, he thought he had no other choice. However, all was not lost. Murthy could still study engineering , but at the local college. His father said he could only afford that much. Murthy agreed, displaying a maturity beyond his age. Not yet past his teens, he understood his father's problems and was ready to sacrifice his dreams for the sake of his family.

'It is a matter of pride to study at the IIT. It is also true that it is a passport to success. But can everyone get that opportunity? If I were to work hard, just as I did for the entrance examination, if I were to use all my talent and endeavour, can't I still set my life on the path to prosperity?' This thought guided him through several years in future.

First brush with a computer

'I must accept what I cannot change, but I won't let circumstances take control of my life. I must overcome the situation and emerge successful.'

Soon he got over the disappointment of not being able to join IIT and took up a BE course at the National Institute of Engineering, affiliated to Mysore University. He chose Electrical Engineering as his subject; here too he had some wonderful teachers and soon became their favourite student. He showed much more interest in his studies than he did in school and learnt many new things with great enthusiasm. In 1967, he stood first when he passed out of college after obtaining his BE degree. Now he had another chance to get into IIT. Fortunately, this time round, he was not disappointed. He joined the M.Tech course at IIT Kanpur and was still eligible for a scholarship that completely took care of his hostel fees.

At IIT, Murthy constantly interacted with students from different parts of India, an experience he enjoyed. Though he specialised in Electrical Engineering, he found that he was attracted to something else — the new computer developed by IBM and imported into India.

This was the first time Murthy saw a computer. When the teachers explained what the magical instrument could do, he listened with astonishment and excitement. He acquired considerable knowledge of computers. Within his two-year stint as a student there he became an expert in the field.

Passion to experiment

In 1969, when he graduated with an M.Tech degree, four big corporations offered him jobs — *Hindustan Machine Tools* (HMT), a leading wrist watch manufacturer, the Government-run *Electronics Corporation of India*, Tata's *TELCO* and *Air India*, the international airline run by the Indian Government.

All these companies offered Murthy high-salaried jobs which could be a challenge to his expertise. Even as he pondered over the options, another golden opportunity came his way. Professor Krishnaiah, whom Murthy had admired greatly during his college days, asked him to join the Indian Institute of Management (IIM) in Ahmedabad as a faculty. Though the salary at IIM would not match up to the salaries offered by the other four companies, Murthy would definitely gain some worthy experience.

First of all, the college atmosphere would lighten the burden of the job; a teacher could feel like a student and work with more enthusiasm. The institute would offer greater opportunities to experiment with and learn new things compared to a commercial establishment. More importantly, a brand new computer was to be installed at the IIM Ahmedabad. He could try out its many functions and gain valuable experience.

Krishnaiah explained all this to Murthy and convinced him. Murthy accepted the offer of joining IIM Ahmedabad as Chief System Programmer in 1969, on a starting salary of Rs 800 per month. Just as he had expected, the new job was helpful to him in several ways; it was equivalent to pursuing higher studies or training in the computer field. Murthy regularly spent nearly 20 hours a day in front of his computer, often returning to his room as late as 3 am. After a short sleep, he invariably got back to work at7 am. Even though he spent a major part of the day with his computer, his love for the machine did not diminish even a little. In fact, it grew by leaps and bounds, and soon he was driven by the passion to experiment.

While working at IIM, Murthy had published a research paper, which drew the attention of several prospective employers. One of the companies that approached him was *SESA* of

France. Murthy joined SESA in 1972 and moved to Paris. He tackled the challenging job with a great deal of enthusiasm, considering it an opportunity to showcase his talent. The years Murthy spent in Paris changed his life totally. He developed clear views about why people should earn money and how they should share it with the rest of the society. According to him, 'A civilised society is one where each generation makes personal sacrifices to ensure a better and happier world for the next generation. Beyond a certain level of comfort I think one's wealth should be seen as an opportunity to make a difference to the society. My colleagues think so too. I have always said that the real power of money is the power to give it away.'

Accordingly, he gave away everything he earned abroad to others in need. He did not keep anything for himself. When he decided to return to India in 1974 after working in France for three years, he had a mere $450 left with him. In 1975, Murthy and one of his college professors started a research establishment called Systems Research Institute (SRI). After working with SRI for two years, Murthy joined Patni Computer Systems (PCS) in Mumbai as a consultant.

Before talking about his stint at PCS, mention should be made about an extraordinary girl he met in Pune. In a way, she was instrumental in Murthy's joining a large firm like Patni. It is an interesting love story!

How Murthy met Sudha

A voracious reader, Sudha used to borrow books from one of her colleagues, Prasanna. She found the name 'Narayana Murthy' written on the first page of most of these books. This sparked her curiosity and she asked Prasanna who this 'Narayana Murthy' was. Prasanna spoke with pride about his friend Narayana Murthy. She learnt that Murthy had returned from Paris and that he was involved in research at SRI. She also learnt of his abiding interest in reading.

Narayana Murthy also belonged to Karnataka as Sudha did. Soon, she developed a special liking and a fellow feeling for Murthy, whom she had not even seen. Sudha had conjured up a certain image of the foreign-returned expert. But when the two finally met amidst a group of friends, she found him quite the opposite of what she had imagined; he had come to meet her wearing ordinary clothes and thick glasses.

Murthy was not too well off, but he was quite an expert at his work. He was bubbling with enthusiasm, ideas and dreams. He was supremely confident and had a clear outlook for the future. This attracted Sudha to him; they met often and soon became good friends.

In August 1977, Murthy joined Patni Computers. The young couple's patient wait yielded sweet fruits, and their wedding was arranged soon. On 10 February, 1978, Sudha and Narayana Murthy's marriage took place in a simple ceremony at Murthy's house in Bangalore.

On the workfront, Murthy grew in stature at Patni. He was in charge of the software section, and inducted many talented young people as new employees thereby infusing new life into the company. The only significant thing that united all these men was that they were not quite happy with their work. Though the job was well-paid, it was not challenging enough to satisfy their hunger for creativity. They felt there was much more than they could do there and had the spark to do something different.

Thus the friends came together and decided to establish a new company that would offer world class software services in India. They wanted to build an organisation that would offer them the best of opportunities. Murthy realised that it would be difficult for India to emerge as a force to reckon with in computer hardware business, and that her development had to be in the software sector.

Those days, it was difficult to import computers into India. But Murthy and his team were confident that they could make it big by developing software for foreign countries and offering offshore computer services from India. This could bring in considerable earnings for them. But that dream of theirs remained unfulfilled due to lack of funds. Every member of the group was at a loss as to what could be done next.

A New Initiative

Back home from work one day, Murthy told Sudha, 'I want to resign from this job and establish a new software company'. Sudha was shocked at this. Though she raised her objections, Murthy was determined to go ahead. He explained that India could look forward to a bright future in the software sector, and that if the country's poverty is to be eradicated, it could be only done by generating wealth. 'This is the right moment. We must somehow or the other, make use of this opportunity,' he said.

Sudha could now see reason in his idea. Still, when life was going on peacefully with a good job and a handsome salary, was this experiment of starting a new company necessary? she wondered, and was worried. But Murthy was clear about his decision. He had great faith in his group. He firmly believed that if all the seven of them worked together with dedication, they could shape up and build an outstanding company.

Now Sudha was in a predicament. Should she support her husband, who had such great faith in his decision or should she make things clear for him and and ask him to continue in the present job for some more time? She could not come to an immediate conclusion. So she asked her husband for more details: 'Are you starting this company alone? Or are there partners?'

'My six friends and I are going to start this venture,' said Murthy, 'We have decided to invest Rs 10,000 each'.

Sudha now asked the next important question: 'What are you going to do for the money?'

'That is where I need your help', said Murthy. 'Will you lend me the money to make my dream come true?'

Treasure in a cupboard

There is always uncertainty in starting a business. When Narayana Murthy said that he was planning to start a new business, these were the thoughts that flashed across Sudha's mind. She had great faith in her husband's expertise. Still, she wondered whether the experiment was necessary at this juncture.

Nevertheless, Sudha also understood that without her cooperation and support, Murthy would not be able to make his dream become a reality. In fact, Murthy needed not just Sudha's cooperation but her money as well.

So, where would they find the Rs 10,000? At that point, Sudha remembered her mother's words. Sudha's mother had advised her to put aside in a grocery container whatever money was left, after meeting the family expenses every month, even if it were a very small amount. Later, when there was some difficult situation, this would come in handy.

When she heard her mother's advice, Sudha was amused as she had firmly believed that they would never face such a difficult situation. Nevertheless, she respected her mother's word as she was experienced in such matters and began saving some money in her kitchen *almirah* (cabinet).

Now that Murthy asked for her help to start a new business, she suddenly remembered the money she had been saving in the *almirah*. Sudha opened the cupboard with great expectations. When she counted the money, there it was — the amount that Murthy actually required!

Now Sudha had to make a tough decision. Was it wise to hand over their only savings to Murthy to invest in his new venture? She once again recalled what her mother had said long ago, 'Spend such savings whenever the necessity arises'.

Sudha felt that it was a moment of absolute necessity. She prayed to her favourite deities and handed over the money to her husband. 'Chase your dreams without any worry. But you have only three years' time,' Sudha told Murthy.

Just like the Rs 10,000 given by Sudha, the three years that Murthy would work hence would be considered his investment in the venture.

Sudha said that she would back him wholeheartedly during those three years, regardless of profit or loss. Murthy approved of her mature decision which gave him sufficient time to make his dream come true, or venture out of it if it turned out to be impractical.

Dream Comes True

At last, when the funds required for the new company were ready, all the seven friends decided to quit Patni at the same time.

The new entrepreneurs were NR Narayana Murthy, Nandan Nilekani, K Dinesh, S Gopalakrishnan, NS Raghavan, SD Shibulal and Ashok Arora. Of them, Raghavan and Murthy were over thirty and the rest were in their mid-twenties. Each person was an expert in his field and the partners were therefore confident about their group. Though they had all resigned by the end of 1980, they could not leave Patni immediately, as they had to complete certain tasks assigned to them before joining their new company.

A huge investment was required to establish a new company, especially that which aimed at competing with well-known companies at the global level. The money that Murthy and his friends had collected was meagre, compared to the investment required for importing modern computers and hiring experts. They realised that they needed much more investment than they had thought, for them to meet global standards.

All the banks that Murthy approached rejected his proposals even without analysing them properly. The software industry would generate huge profits in return, on the massive investments made in it. But no one realised it at that point of time and no one wanted to believe it.

At this juncture, Murthy happened to meet KSN Narayana Murthy, who was then Chairman of Karnataka State. In the early 1980s, the software industry in India was still in its formative years. Infosys suffered the consequences of thinking ahead of time. Though its ideas and objectives were admirable, it could not manage to have the basic facilities required for a business.

While Infosys took roots in Pune, Murthy's family lived in Mumbai. Initially Murthy stayed in Mumbai and travelled frequently to Pune. However, the recurrent trips took their toll on Murthy, both physically and economically. So he decided to look for a house in Pune.

Infosys was not affluent enough to rent office space separately. So his plan was to look for a house to stay in and use it as an office too. Similarly, it was not possible, in the beginning, to recruit anyone to work in Infosys, as they could not afford to pay salaries. For a while, the seven men had to take on various *avatars* such as boss, salesman, computer expert and consultant, all at the same time.

Fortunately, all the seven partners worked hard without any distraction. Such trivial things and small woes did not perturb them. Not only they but also their wives had to make sacrifices. For instance, Sudha undertook several tasks for Infosys during her spare time, from writing computer programs to making tea for the staff, answering the telephone and replying to letters. For both Sudha and Murthy, it was a difficult period.

Sudha gave birth to a baby girl in her home town, Hubli. Happy with the arrival of their new baby, Murthy and Sudha named her Akshatha. Due to the unfazed and continued efforts of Murthy and his friends, Infosys had grown to some extent. In order to help them, Sudha resigned her job with Telco and move to Pune. For this, she had to meet the chairman of the Tata group, JRD Tata. He asked her, 'Why are you resigning your job?'

Sudha replied, 'My husband has started a new business. I have decided to help him.'

'Very good,' said JRD Tata and appreciated her decision. Then he asked, 'You have started a new business; what will you do with the profits you make from it?'

This question sounded strange to Sudha. Infosys had just started and how could she think about profits now? But JRD Tata's views were quite different.

'Whatever business we start, we ought to have the conviction that we will make profit from it. If such a conviction is not there, it is a waste to get involved in it. We must give back the profit to the society from which we make it,' he said.

Sudha still remembers that advice. It made a deep impression on her and encouraged her to get involved in many social service projects.

Swimming against the Tide

Murthy insisted that their first duty is to supply good quality software to their clients at a reasonable price. He formulated three major principles for the company.

'First, whatever software we write, we must satisfy the expectations of our clients in all aspects. By using the software written or sold by us, they must get added competitive advantage and value.'

'Second, whatever we do, it must not target any specific country or area. Our prospective clients could be in different countries. We must create only globalised software.' 'Third, there should be no compromise in the quality of our software service. We must always offer professional and quality service acceptable to all, without complaints.'

Murthy believed that by following these three principles, Infosys could supply international quality software services from India. But then, there was the cost advantage to look into. 'The expenditure is far less in our country, compared to other countries. As what we charge our clients will also be lower, the respect for India would also grow at the global level very soon. Thereafter, opportunities would increase for such services here also.' This was his long-term plan.

Infosys focussed on the foreign market and worked hard to earn a name in the countries with a lot of opportunities for software services. The company found interested and prospective clients and instilled confidence in them that it could supply whatever they expected.

None of the founders of Infosys, including Murthy, had any idea of settling abroad. But having decided that Infosys was to concentrate on foreign market, what was the point in continuing to stay in India? Leaving Murthy behind to take care of the work here, the rest of them went to the US and stayed there. After sustained efforts by the Infosys team, Data Basics from New York showed interest in using

Infosys's services. When an agreement was signed, it opened new doors for Infosys and it started growing.

Meanwhile, in India, Murthy faced as many problems as the Infosys representatives in America faced. The Indian Government did not function at the same pace that his thought process did.

Positive attitude during testing times

At that point of time, the Government did not know or understand or explore the possibilities for the development of computer science. The very industry was not given any facilities or concessions, and had to seek the Government's help for everything.

For example, if a new company wanted to import a computer, the Government regulations made it a long and complicated process. It would be years before they could get officials to sign a letter granting them permission to import the required computer. These regulations delayed Murthy's work and plans inordinately. So Infosys had to share computers on a contract basis with another company.

Till Infosys obtained permission to import the computer in 1984, most of the software work was done on borrowed computers. Another problem was the lack of a phone connection, especially embarrassing and inconvenient while approaching foreign companies for business. Long before it had its own telephone connection, Infosys made its business calls from a public booth at the corner of the street. In case of an emergency or during troubleshooting, Infosys sent its representative in person, which naturally escalated the company's expenses; but it had no other choice.

Murthy sweated it out riding a bicycle everywhere, even to meet important persons. He also had to travel to various cities for business. Since these always cropped up suddenly, and one after another, he had to travel without any respite. His only aim was to raise the Infosys banner to every opportunity that came by. And despite all its problems, Infosys did earn some profit in the first year.

Murthy faced considerable difficulties, but with a positive attitude. He said, 'Only because the Government regulations harassed us so much, we got the courage to swim against the tide even during very difficult times. Due to that, we became efficient managers and rose above all good people'.

Chalo Bangalore!

Murthy and his friends decided to move Infosys to Bangalore, based on three reasons:

First, compared to North India, there were more engineering colleges in the South and the quality of education also had an edge. So Murthy and his partners felt that when Infosys developed further, they had better chances of hiring superior manpower in the South.

Second, the expenses were higher in Mumbai and Pune. Infosys could save money and earn more profit for the investors by moving to a cheaper city, with adequate infrastructure and connectivity to service their foreign clients.

Murthy was far-sighted and perceptive, and Infosys was the first software company in Bangalore. Many local and foreign companies followed suit, taking advantage of the facilities available at Bangalore at that time. It is a different thing that Bangalore later became as expensive a city as Mumbai.

The third important reason was that MICO (Motor Industries Company Limited) was based in Bangalore.

In 1983, Murthy and Infosys shifted to Bangalore. Considering the status of Infosys at that point, the MICO contract, valued at around Rs 1.25 crore, was a bulky order. When the time came for Murthy and NS Raghavan to sign the agreement, they rushed to the MICO office on a friend's scooter, as they could not find an autorickshaw in time. Vikram Bhatt, who was then a director of MICO, was taken aback. 'At least next time rent a car,' he advised them.

Meanwhile, Sudha gave birth to a baby boy, Rohan, in Hubli. At the same time, Murthy was away from home, in the US on work. So for about a year he could not see his son. After Murthy's return from the US, Infosys found a few new clients besides MICO. Everyone had to work for longer hours and Infosys was beginning to earn the respect and attention of the Indian software industry.

At this point, Sudha wanted to resign her job and join Infosys. Most of the directors of the company, who felt that her induction into the group as a director would strengthen Infosys, welcomed the move, but opposition came from totally unexpected quarters.

Murthy said she should not join Infosys. 'You may decide it for yourself; only one of us can continue to work in this company. The other has to leave. I don't want to force you in any way. If you wish to continue here, I am willing to leave'.

Sudha could not understand. Astonished at this, she looked at him and said, 'We both have the experience and the technical knowledge to work in this company'.

'I know that. But anyone working here needs to be totally involved without any other work or temptations; only then can this company at its nascent stage come up,' said Murthy.

'So what? Why do you think we two cannot work together?'

'If both husband and wife begin to work for the company, then who would look after the home and children?' asked Murthy. 'Do you think I am happy to say this? But for the sake of our family, one of us has to make this sacrifice.'

His wife could not decline his argument. She understood that, as Murthy said, it would be right only if one of them took care of the family and the other worked for Infosys with involvement. So she gave up her desire to join Infosys, though half-heartedly. Having been pushed into this unwilling decision, how did she manage to achieve so much?

It is here that Sudha's great determination and self-confidence come through. She did not lose her sense of individuality even when she resigned her job and when the circumstances did not allow her to join Infosys. Her life has been an example of confidence building.

Sudha took care of the home and children, and renewed her interest in writing. She has written more than ten books in Kannada — novels, essays, travelogues and introductory books on computers — many of which have been translated into Tamil, English, Malayalam and Telugu. She undertook social work through Infosys Trust and took to teaching whenever time permitted.

The Door Opens

In the 1980s, Murthy and other Infosys founders worked hard, in spite of many problems, to develop the company. A couple of companies like Infosys were also progressing slowly. They had to face many restrictions and regulations with respect to the foreign market, and this slowed down the company's growth considerably.

During this time, other companies involved in similar businesses came forward to buy Infosys. Some of the founders of Infosys argued that it was wiser to sell off the company than struggle on a daily basis. But Murthy had great faith in Infosys and was adamant that they 'should not sell themselves. The argument went on for almost five hours.'

'We can't continue to face losses. Let us sell the company immediately,' said some, while others said, 'it is cowardice to withdraw in such circumstances; we must continue to run the company'.

Murthy heard everyone out and declared, 'If you have confidence in our group stay with me. Otherwise, instead of some other person buying our company, I'll buy all your shares myself.' There was total silence. While everyone was wondering how to respond to this proposal, Murthy continued, 'It is indeed difficult to run such a company successfully in our country. Nevertheless, I am fully convinced that we can overcome all these problems'.

The argument ended there. Their respect for Murthy was such that all the Infosys partners shed their fears and reiterated their total faith in him. They agreed to work with a lot more fervour and devotion. An unwritten resolution was passed that there would never ever be any talk about closing their company or selling it.

Murthy often used to say, 'Starting and running a business is not like running a 100-metres' race, it is like a marathon'. One should not sprint away in a wink; one must build up the ability and an untiring mind to run continuously for hours together, mile after mile, in order to succeed'. Murthy practically proved his point with Infosys. It became one of the best companies of India in the next few years.

The company's turning point came when the Congress Government formed in 1991 under Narasimha Rao and, the then finance minister, Manmohan Singh was supportive with their economic reforms.

Starting with India's export-import policy, all the regulations regarding foreign trade were relaxed and open trade developed. Because of these economic reforms Indians got opportunities to go abroad and foreign companies decided to invest here. Infosys did not lose any time in taking advantage of these opportunities.

The companies did not have to wait long for any permission and also did not have to run to Delhi for everything. The business formalities that took eight months to a year earlier, could now be completed in a day or two. Similarly, the Reserve Bank's regulations regarding foreign travel were also relaxed. Earlier, it was mandatory to wait five to ten days after applying to RBI when one wanted to go abroad for business. But after 1991, it became possible to fly abroad within a day.

As mentioned earlier, after 1991, many foreign companies got the opportunity to invest in India. The cost of establishing a business in India was much less compared to other countries. This made well-known companies of developed nations like the US look at the possibility of establishing their branches in India. They opened their offices in all the important cities of India, invested in millions, and gave open invitations to intelligent youngsters to come and join them. As a result, software experts in local firms like Infosys began migrating to foreign companies looking for better salaries, better facilities and opportunities to go abroad.

Under these circumstances, Murthy and his partners went into a huddle. One solution for the current problem was to approach the Government immediately and request it to take measures to prevent the foreign companies from entering the country. At this point of time, Murthy was the chairman of NASSCOM, the association of Indian software service industries. If he wished, he could have pleaded with the Government that business was being affected and therefore foreign software companies should be barred from entering India.

But Murthy did not want to do so. He wanted to succeed on the strength of their skills and not by preventing others from functioning. Therefore, he felt other strategies must be followed to enable the company to grow, and to stop the employees, particularly youngsters, from jumping ship.

Accordingly, it was decided that they would find out why the youngsters were moving to other companies and offer them the same facilities and concessions they would get elsewhere. In short, all provisions would be made to keep the employees happy and make sure that they didn't even think of moving out.

This idea seems very simple; but Infosys was the first establishment to think in this manner. Only because it respected its employees and considered their welfare important, was it able to overcome the crisis effectively.

Right from the beginning, Murthy treated both the founders and other members of Infosys equally. He used to say, 'Those working hard throughout the day will feel tired when they go home in the evening. But when they come to work the next day, they must work with the same old enthusiasm.' It means that everyone should be given salaries and other perks as per their efforts. They should be able to enjoy the outcome of their work with total satisfaction.

This idea of Murthy's, which approached the problem with sensitivity and based on psychology, yielded immediate results. The salaries and perks of Infosys employees were raised to the level of the other companies, or even more. In addition, Infosys took pains in creating an excellent working environment.

Accordingly, in 1993-94, Infosys constructed a huge office building in Bangalore with all the facilities. This building became an icon of great achievement for Infosys, which began its business in a small two-room house in Pune.

The Bangalore head office of Infosys is spread over 50 acres of land. It is the largest software campus in the world. On this sprawling campus, which appears like a mini city, in addition to offices, there are other facilities like tennis court, golf link, swimming pool, gymnasium and restaurants to make the employees comfortable during their leisure hours.

But were these enough? When Infosys raised the salaries by Rs 10, if the competitor announced a hike of Rs 100, what should be done?

A revolutionary scheme

As an extension of this thought, for the first time in India, Murthy brought in a revolutionary scheme — all the employees of a company would share the development and profits of the company — it was known as ESOP or Employees Stock Option Plan[1].

This scheme was very new to India though it was being followed in many successful American companies. All the new financial companies of America, known as Silicon Valley companies, were retaining their employees only through ESOP.

Accordingly, stock options of the company were given to Infosys employees and even the new recruits. These were not full shares, and were known as options. That is, after a specific period, the company shares could be bought at a previously mentioned strike price. At that time whatever might be the share price in the market, the shares could be bought at the price agreed upon earlier and sold at a profit in the open market.

By this arrangement, Infosys would distribute a certain percentage of its profits to each of its employee. Infosys was the first Indian software company to happily share its profits with everyone instead of locking it up. As a result, the dividing line between the employer and employee faded to some extent, and the employees developed a feeling of attachment and loyalty to the company.

It was a time when the Infosys banner was flying high in the Indian and international software markets. The company's share value increased, and many Infosys members became very rich. When competent computer experts were happily jumping from one company to another elsewhere, very few quit Infosys.

In 1993, Infosys obtained the quality certificate, 'ISO 9001'. The very next year, a large-scale expansion of its services was planned. Infosys offices were opened in all the major cities of India. Soon, they expanded their business by

---

[1] The ESOP scheme, which enabled the sharing of the profits of Infosys, was stopped in 2004.

opening offices abroad, for which a great number of new recruits were employed.

Infosys' strength grew, so did its profit. From 1994 to 1997, the profit of Infosys increased three-folds. But is piling profit alone the objective of a company? Doesn't it have any other social commitments?

Social bent of mind

There was a time, when attracted by the Communist ideology, Murthy had given away most of the money he had saved in Paris, and returned to India empty-handed. Only after that did he establish Infosys, which became one of India's largest software empires that employed several educated youngsters.

At the time of his establishing Infosys, the most important thought in Murthy's mind was to bring in wealth into the country. He firmly believed that only after this would it be possible to distribute money equally to the needy.

Therefore, in the mid-1990s when Infosys had grown into a very big enterprise, Murthy wanted to divert his attention to service-oriented activities for those at the lowest rung of the society. While talking about it, he had said, 'However successful a company might be, if it does not have a sense of social responsibility, its success cannot be total'.

However good the Government might be, in a large country like India with the world's second largest population, it is not possible to expect equal distribution of wealth and other basic amenities. Starting from the basic needs like food, clothes, shelter, proper medical facilities and education, the long list remained an unfulfilled dream for many. Because of this, the disparity between the rich and the poor kept widening. If this sad situation were to be changed, the haves had to extend a helping hand to the have-nots. This was Murthy's view with regard to the society.

Like Murthy, the other founders and partners of Infosys were also interested in the welfare of the society. Therefore, with everybody's consent some important plans were charted out. But in order to implement them, a strong set up and great involvement were essential. Only then could they make sure that the money spent went to the needy without being wasted.

So they decided to found a Trust for social service, as a sister concern of Infosys. Murthy's wife Sudha was chosen to head the Trust. Right from her childhood, Sudha had grown up with an inclination towards charity. Sudha was already attracted by the ideologies of Mahatma Gandhi and Gautama Buddha. She did not forget JRD Tata's advice too.

In December 1996, the Infosys Foundation was established. It was a non-profitable organisation set up for the service and support of the most backward in the society, particularly women and children. The Foundation began its work with NS Raghavan and Sudha Gopalakrishnan, who were also keenly interested in social service, and extended a helping hand to Sudha Narayana Murthy.

Infosys Foundation reached out to the most backward villages in India, set up hospitals and schools, and provided computers, libraries and other basic facilities. It offered monetary help to meritorious students and founded homes for the destitute. Sudha now travels around the country, meets different kinds of people and listens to their problems. Based on this information, service is rendered to the needy.

Murthy talks about the Foundation with pride. 'The benefits should reach everyone at various strata of the society. Therefore, we set aside a certain part of our earnings for such useful work.'

The Foundation, functioning under the leadership of Sudha for the past 12 years, has won some prestigious awards. She has won over 20 awards from India and abroad for social service. But all these accolades have not made Sudha and Murthy rest on their laurels. They want to continue their work and stick to their simple lifestyle as always.

Murthy is fondly known as 'Corporate Gandhi'. Do you know why? Read on…

Simplicity as a way of life

After the success of Infosys, Narayana Murthy was listed as one of the richest Indian in the world. But even now, Murthy and Sudha live in an ordinary flat in an apartment block in Bangalore's Jayanagar area. They have no servants or cooks to assist them. As far as possible, Sudha takes care of the cooking and other household chores; Murthy also lends a helping hand now and then.

But why should the founder of one of India's biggest private enterprises live such a simple life? Why can't they employ someone at least for cleaning the house and cooking? Such questions have been put to the couple often. 'We earn money for our day-to-day needs. But once those needs have been fulfilled, it becomes meaningless to earn more, especially after a point of time. Therefore, we consider spending such extra earnings as an opportunity for making social changes and serving fellow human beings,' Murthy said.

Annually, on behalf of Infosys, about Rs 5 crores is spent on welfare schemes and projects for the needy. The entire amount goes through the Infosys Foundation to the poor, the destitute, deserving students and abandoned women and children in various villages, towns and hilly areas (colder regions) of India.

Murthy, who is supporting and funding these schemes, is quietly engaged in another important social service. Wishing to improve the quality of higher education in India, he is helping educational institutions in various ways. His aim is to bring back the 'golden age,' when higher studies in our country was considered very good and respectable, by preventing them from slowly losing their value and by improving the quality of higher education.

Murthy, who realised the importance of higher education, has established an excellent educational institution for the employees of his company. This training centre, called the Infosys Leadership Institute, helps to develop the leadership qualities of the Infosys family. At this centre, people ranging from the founder to the driver have undergone training, and have improved their leadership qualities. This centre is creating the next-generation leaders for Infosys.

Leadership, according to Murthy, is to complete with determination a job, which others avoid considering it impossible. Infosys has many such people who have realised this, and this is reason enough for the company to take majestic strides even when faced with problems.

Role models

Many Indians, ranging from business magnates and entrepreneurs to young students, consider Murthy and Sudha as their role models. In fact, in the last ten years, theirs is the biggest success story. The two have made significant contributions in the areas of pioneering use of technology, creating numerous job opportunities, saving money and towards social service.

Attracted a lot by the Gandhian philosophy, Murthy has fashioned his social life based on the great man's principles. Shy by nature, he would never hurt anyone with words and no one can anger him in any situation. He would never compromise on quality, and treats his employees with great respect. When his wife, relatives or members of Infosys families do something just noticeable, he would still shower praise on them whole-heartedly; and if the work done is extraordinary, his praise would be limitless. It is the lack of complacency that has taken him to great heights. Even now, when Infosys has become one of the biggest companies of India, Murthy still calls it a 'developing company'.

In spite of being one of the seven founders of Infosys, and a guiding force behind its growth, he holds less than 10% of its shares. Because of this, there is no disparity between employer and employees, and the company is like one big family. If an attendant brought in something to drink while Murthy was busy talking to an important visitor, he would introduce him as 'his colleague'.

Murthy is very pious by nature. According to him, 'Only when we face difficult situations, our faith and respect for God increases. Similarly, whenever something good happens to me, I believe it is God's grace.'

Murthy also believes in the epithet, 'Work is Divine'. Living in a simple apartment, his day begins very early. He gets busy soon after with household work and *pooja*. After that, if there is time, he does a little gardening. Then, he is off to work by 6 am, either by car or by the company bus. He reaches office by around 6.30 am daily, and works for about 15 hours a day, i.e., almost 90 hours a week. Therefore, he rarely gets any leisure time. Even on such rare occasions, he spends time listening to music. Just like his father, he is very much interested in Western Classical music and has over a thousand tapes and discs in his collection. Murthy is equally interested in books. Every month, a major portion of his expenditure goes towards buying books.

Another distinctive feature everyone admires in Murthy is his desire not to lose his Indian identity, even after becoming a big businessman. That is why he never hesitates to speak in public about his personal life or his faith in God.

According to Murthy, every Indian lives a double life striving to be a responsible head of the family and also holds a busy portfolio at office, and tries to manage both the roles efficiently.

For some, it becomes difficult to decide which role is more important and how to function within the parameters of contemporary lifestyle, and at the same time not lose sight of our tradition and culture. For such people, Murthy's life and the success of Infosys appear to be ideal examples to follow.

Moulding the future

Murthy believes that today's youth are the future architects of India. He says that students and youngsters should always remain grateful to the three powers which created them — parents, teachers and the motherland.

Murthy has great respect for his teachers. His evolution came from institutions like the IIT and IIM where he had excellent teachers. He has approached his teachers on various occasions to take important decisions in his life. Perhaps this is why Murthy is very much interested in teaching. Many people, who have moved closely with him, have mentioned that though he is a businessman, he is an educationist at heart. Whenever Murthy finds the time he makes it a point to talk to students. Whether they are students of the first standard or those on the verge of completing higher studies, he approaches them with respect.

Murthy's important advice to students is: 'Improve your skills as much as possible. You must evolve into experts to be respected and noticed by the entire world; while you earn your expertise, you will also earn money, fame and other honours automatically. But most importantly, through you, the respect for our country should grow. It is your duty.'

Murthy, who is a responsible guide and an ideal example for the next generation, considers two famous persons as his role models — Mahatma Gandhi and Singapore leader Lee Kuan Yew.

Murthy has voiced his concern for various social problems: 'In these many years since our Independence there is so much advancement in our country — we have established many industries, we have sent rockets and satellites soaring into the sky. But all of them have not got their basic necessities.' Murthy is worried that India has not developed its human resources properly. 'We have not created good leaders. That is the biggest problem!'

Regarding his dream, Murthy says: 'Every child born in India must get enough food, proper medical facilities, housing and education.'

Similarly, in business, he feels that Indian products and services should be valued as the best at the global level. Indian industries should be upgraded till they reach that level of global competitiveness. 'Our country has skills in abundance; but we must find the impediments to our growth and destroy them. We must observe the other developed countries, learn the secret of their success and change our mindset accordingly.'

Murthy has always dreamt of making India one of the best countries in the world.

'World class' services

In 1993, Infosys issued its shares for the first time, priced at Rs 95. It increased to Rs 13,952 at the beginning of 1999, making a huge profit that was more than 146 times the original value. Since then, Infosys has grown in leaps and bounds, but the year 1999 remains a milestone year. The public and business experts, who were looking at Infosys as 'just one of the companies that were doing well' till then, began to look up to it with awe.

The annual income of Infosys had reached $100 million in 1999, and grew to reach $1 billion in 2004. In Indian terms, the income through software services in 2003-04 was Rs 4,760 crores and in the subsequent year it was Rs 6,860 crores.

Infosys, which began with just seven people in a small room, now has offices in all the major cities of India and in many countries with over 1,00,000 employees on its rolls. A major portion of its income comes from its foreign clients. Therefore, from the beginning, as Murthy has been insisting, Infosys software and its relevant services function with the objective of being 'world class'.

But what makes Infosys a 'world class' company earning an annual income of Rs 16,692 crores?

Murthy often says that the future of Infosys depends on the younger generation of the country. With this view in mind, and also considering the long-term development of Infosys, Murthy decided to do something for the next generation. To facilitate the growth of fresh, young talent, he stepped down from the post of Chief Executive Officer of Infosys on 31 March, 2002. Another founder of Infosys, Nandan Nilekani has taken over as the CEO. Murthy continues to function as the chairman and mentor of the company.

Murthy may have decided to give room to new leaders, new efforts and new ideas, but his experience is still essential in making Infosys a household name at the global level. At an age when most Indians retire from employment and look forward to rest and relax, Murthy is still active working as a brand ambassador and the public face of Infosys.

What impels him to work continuously like this? Murthy responds to this question with a small example. In the world of sports, winning the game is what matters. Losers do not have any place in a team or in the field. The real reward for a player is when he keeps winning.

'Similarly, happiness in life is not at the place we reach, but in the journey to that place,' concludes Narayana Murthy.

Prodigy books

Biographies

Abdul Kalam
Charles Darwin
Marie Curie
Visvesvaraya
Srinivasa Ramanujan
Newton
Einstein
James Watt
Jagdish Chandra Bose
Alexander Graham Bell
Gandhi
Jawaharlal Nehru
Mother Teresa
Ambedkar
Bhagat Sigh
Tipu Sultan
Rani of Jhansi
Akbar
Shivaji
Bharati
Martin Luther King
Alexander the Great
Napoleon
Adolf Hitler
Charlie Chaplin
Walt Disney
Bill Gates
Narayana Murthy

Classics Retold

Homer's Iliad
The Odyssey
The Tempest
Hamlet
The Merchant of Venice
Twelfth Night
Romeo and Juliet
Macbeth

Other Titles

The Universe
Hinduism
Global Warming
Abraham Lincoln
The New 7 wonders of the World
Life
Tsunami
Dinosaurs
Ganga
World War II
Madras - Chennai
Exam Tips
The Internet

www.ingramcontent.com/pod-product-compliance
Lightning Source LLC
Chambersburg PA
CBHW031425160726
47993CB00003B/1396